Mount St. Helens
and Other Volcanoes of the West

Mount St. Helens
and Other Volcanoes of the West

Concept and Design: Robert D. Shangle
Text: Linda Kelso

First Printing October, 1980
Published by Beautiful America Publishing Company
P.O. Box 608, Beaverton, Oregon 97075
Robert D. Shangle, Publisher

ISBN 0-89802-202-9

Photo Credits

ROY BISHOP—*page 86; page 98; page 119.*

JAMES BLANK—*page 69; pages 76-77; page 107; pages 116-117.*

BOB CLEMENZ—*pages 72-73.*

ED COOPER—*pages 88-89; page 90; pages 108-109.*

DON EASTMAN—*page 67; page 137.*

MIKE EPSTEIN—*page 95.*

DAVID FALCONER—*page 22; page 30; page 38.*

AL HAYWARD—*page 24; page 25; page 26; page 32; page 43; page 50; page 54; page 58; page 59; page 60; page 61.*

JOHN HILL—*pages 20-21; page 78; pages 92-93; page 105; page 106; page 114; pages 124-125; page 128.*

EVERETT HURST—*page 19.*

PAT AND TOM LEESON—*page 23.*

MIKE LLOYD—*page 48, page 62.*

NGHIA MAC—*page 63.*

HUGH MCKENNA—*page 99.*

ANCIL NANCE—*page 35; page 39; page 45; page 49; page 51; page 57.*

LEWIS NELSON—*page 31; pages 36-37; page 44; page 52; page 53; page 55; page 83; page 87; page 91; page 96; page 103; page 110; page 112; page 115; page 118.*

PAT O'HARA—*page 66; page 70; page 94; pages 132-133.*

OREGON STATE HIGHWAY DEPARTMENT—*page 104; page 111.*

H.G. SCHLICKER—*page 74; page 127; page 140.*

ROBERT SHANGLE—*page 18; page 80; page 113; page 141.*

DONALD TEAGUE—*page 68.*

STEVE TERRILL—*page 17; page 27; page 28; page 29; page 33; page 34; pages 40-41; page 42; page 46; page 47; page 56; page 64; page 65; page 75; page 79; page 81; page 82; pages 84-85; page 97; pages 100-101; page 102; pages 120-121; page 126; page 136.*

BRUCE AND SAM WHITE—*page 71; page 122; page 123.*

Contents

The Changing Landscape

Created by fire, sculpt by wind and water, our planet is ever changing and ever evolving. Indeed, it will continue to change—and be changed—as long as it exists.

It is easy to think of United States' land as finished and complete—to think the violent forces that change the earth must happen somewhere else—most likely in some primitive faraway place, and to people who are not nearly so civilized, who, like the land they live on, are still maturing.

Volcanoes—those fire-breathing mountains—inspire visions of leaping, twisting tongues of flaming lava thrust high into the air, only to fall and chase hapless innocents down mountainsides. Volcanoes stir up remembrances of myths and old movies of heroes rescuing fair maidens from witch doctors bent on appeasing angry gods with human sacrifices. Of the unfortunates buried at Pompeii, or in our own time, the rain of black ash on Surtsey. But a volcano in the United States—in 1980?

On May 18, 1980, Mount St. Helens, a beautiful cone-shaped peak in southwestern Washington state, 45 miles northeast of Portland, Oregon, erupted with such violence that its blast destroyed 156 square miles of timber in a fan-shaped swatch. Mudslides raced down the mountain's river valleys and tore out seven bridges along the Toutle River. The heat and force of the blast killed many people who were in the area—many of them camped far enough away that they fully expected to be safe from anything that occurred on the mountain. One-and-a-half cubic miles of the mountain were blown out: pulverized into rock, pebbles, ash, and dust. A mushroom-shaped cloud ascended to 63,000 feet and swept eastward, raining ash and other volcanic debris on most of three states.

Mount St. Helens was 9,677 feet high, a major peak of the Cascade Range in Washington state, a graceful cone sometimes called "The Fujiyama of the West," and almost always called "she"—a reference not at all related to her obviously feminine name, but to her distinctly feminine appearance, as compared to the glacier-carved, weathered shapes of other mountains.

Geologists knew her to be a volcano and had even predicted she would erupt sometime before the end of the 20th century. But they did not predict the immensity of what would happen when she did.

The May 18th eruption was one of the most powerful explosions ever witnessed by man—the largest explosion of the century in North America. Magma, hot molten rock, had collected in a pocket far beneath her. Volcanic gasses had accumulated in the magma, creating incredible pressure. The magma welled up inside the mountain, and finally the pressure could no longer be contained. No one alive today had ever witnessed such a blast. It tore asunder a mountain, casting the parts hundreds of miles away, ultimately to affect millions of lives, in one way or another.

For several hours of that once serene Sunday, hell broke out in that little corner of the earth. The dominions of Satan were spewed forth to incinerate everything and everyone in the way. It was an explosion akin to 50 large ocean freighters full of TNT, all going up at once, and more than 500 times as powerful as the atomic bomb dropped on Hiroshima at the end of the Second World War.

The cloud of ash, suspended in steam and gasses, rose to 63,000 feet above the mountain, through three layers of rain clouds, and swept north and east like an angry plague. It blackened the sky, turning day into night. Visibility fell to zero and electronically controlled street lights went on. Planes were grounded. Streets, roads, machinery, and lungs were soon clogged with the gritty, pervasive dust. A covering of ash, measured anywhere from feet to inches, soon accumulated beneath the route of the cloud. A DC-9 commercial aircraft, flying at 33,000 feet, flew four minutes through the ash cloud and was forced to land with clogged engines. Rail, air, and highway travelers were trapped throughout central and eastern Washington, Idaho, and Montana. Ultimately, 1,100 miles of highway in eastern Washington alone would be closed until the ash could be removed.

Trees fell in the direction of the blast, flattened like so many toothpicks. Aerial photos bring to mind slivers of iron neatly lined up in the direction of magnetism. The once beautiful Spirit Lake disappeared in a massive avalanche of rock and mud.

Heat melted glacial ice and snow, and it cascaded downward, mixing with soil and ash. Mud, thus created, swept up everything in its path—rocks, timber, the artifacts of civilization—mixing and grinding it all into a churning mass that tumbled into valleys and thence into rivers.

The Toutle River and its tributaries drain the north and west flanks of the mountain. Into both the north and south forks of the Toutle went millions of tons of mud and debris.

Timber, sucked up in the mud, floated to the top and rafted down the racing current, smashing into bridges. The growing mud flow rocketed down the river valley, cutting new channels, spilling over banks, gathering up still more debris. It spread out over low-lying areas, flooded campgrounds, logging camps, and homes. It caught up log trucks and smashed them around, tossing them to land, bent and broken, in heaps like so many children's toys abandoned in a thunderstorm.

A wall of mud surged on down the Toutle River Valley and knocked out every bridge for 30 miles. Hot ash and gasses warmed the water to probably over 90 degrees Fahrenheit in the immediate vicinity of the blast. The heat, and suspended debris, which literally smothered them, killed all the fish in the river.

The mud and silt was carried down the Toutle to the Cowlitz River and to the Columbia River. By Monday, May 19, the ocean-shipping channel in the Columbia, normally a minimum of 40 feet deep, was clogged with silt to about 18 feet, making ocean shipping impossible.

On the north face of the mountain, a pyroclastic flow—rock and ash suspended in hot gas—rushed down the side at possibly 100 miles per hour, incinerating everything in its path. Such a flow may be as hot as 1,500 degrees Fahrenheit.

Lightning, created by friction between the hot air of the blast and the surrounding cold air, crackled around the crater and about the summit. Along with hot ash, it started as many as 200 forest fires, many of which were smothered by ash. Others were left to burn as firefighters dared not come near. In weeks to come, Forest Service firefighters would attempt to extinguish blazes caused by smoldering timber buried in ash.

Mount St. Helens was left 1,277 feet shorter. Thirty-one people are known, or presumed to be, dead. Hundreds were left homeless, many jobless. At least 5,000 travelers had been stranded. Several major cities in central and eastern Washington, Idaho, and Montana were left to dig out of a coating of powdery, slick, fluid volcanic ash.

And a beautiful mountain was robed in black.

Volcanoes

The name volcano derives from the mythical Roman god, Vulcan, the god of fire and craftsmanship. Ancient peoples either feared or revered the volatile mountains as gods or the instruments of gods. Now we understand that our planet is continually building and changing—and volcanoes are one of the principal instruments of that change.

Scientists agree that the earth is comprised of a thin, 20-mile-deep crust of rock around a thick, 1,800-mile-deep mantle of fluid rock surrounding a dense, heavy iron core.

Most geologists now adhere to the theory that the crust is broken in a series of continent-sized plates that "float" on the molten mantle beneath them. The plates beneath the oceans differ markedly from those bearing continents. Oceanic plates are thinner, but denser and heavier than continental plates. The continually shifting plates move away from one another in some places and crash into each other elsewhere. It is where these plates collide that some of the geological violence, which produces earthquakes and volcanoes, occurs.

A volcano is a place where magma, molten rock from the interior of the earth, is expelled through a vent to the surface. When an oceanic plate and a continental plate collide, the thinner, heavier oceanic plate may plunge beneath the lighter continental plate. The leading edge of the sinking plate bends into the hot mantle below the crust and melts. On the underside of the continental plate is a series of chambers, hollow pockets into which magma rises. Gasses trapped in the magma expand, and when they do, great pressure builds in the chamber. Eventually, the pressure can no longer be contained, the magma erupts through the crust at a weak spot, and a volcano is born. The channel through which the eruption occurs is called a vent. Once a volcanic vent exists, magma from the chamber beneath it will usually continue to erupt through that vent when sufficient pressure builds to cause an eruption.

All volcanic eruptions are not violent. In fact, most volcanoes pop and sizzle at irregular intervals, and the truly cataclysmic, explosive eruptions occur infrequently enough to be notable.

And not all volcanoes are violent. Those of the Cascades are considered to be explosive—that is, they tend to erupt violently and sometimes explosively. But there is a second type of volcano, one from which a thinner, freer flowing lava extrudes almost continually, flowing away from the vent in long sheets. This type of extrusion builds a wide sloping mountain which, because it resembles an upturned warrior's shield when seen from the air, is called a shield volcano. Since the emanation of lava is comparatively constant, the kind of pressure that creates the explosive eruptions for which volcanoes are famous, does not occur. Hawaii's Mauna Loa is a shield volcano.

Of the 529 known active volcanoes in the world today, 421 are located around the perimeter of the Pacific Ocean in what is commonly called the Ring of Fire. This circle of geological violence exists because the Pacific Ocean is spreading.

Volcanoes are not all bad, although sometimes their violent destruction is. They are the principal instruments of earth's recycling—the old rock and sediment gathered on the ocean floor, remelted to become the new land of tomorrow. They create new land that will become fertile farmland for agriculture; rugged peaks that shape the weather; calderas that cradle lovely lakes; hot water that is the source of potential geothermal energy; new river valleys, and fresh, new landscape to delight and challenge man.

Around the World

While volcanic activity around the world is continual, few explode with the violence evidenced by Mount St. Helens.

In the middle of the 15th century, B.C., the entire Minoan civilization, on an island in the Aegean Sea, abruptly vanished from the face of the earth. Scholars now believe its disappearance was attributable to the destruction wrought when Mount Thera, on the island of Santorini some 70 miles distant, blew up. A layer of ash 100 feet thick is thought to have been left by this eruption.

One of history's most famous volcanic eruptions is that of Italy's Mount Vesuvius in 79 A.D. The city of Pompeii at its base was quickly buried in ash, but geologists now believe it was the nueé ardente, or glowing avalanche of gas-charged lava, that killed the Pompeiians. Such flows of debris, suspended in hot gasses, race down the sides of volcanoes in minutes, riding a cushion of compressed air.

A similar phenomenon killed the 30,000 inhabitants of the village of St. Pierre on Martinique in the West Indies. On May 8, 1902, in a violent eruption presaged by over two weeks of intense volcanic activity, a nueé ardente overcame the villagers in just minutes, leaving only one survivor, a prisoner who was confined in a cell with one small window.

Krakatoa, a small island in the Sundra Strait between Java and Sumatra, is part of the Ring of Fire. Starting at 10:02 a.m. on August 27, 1883, in the most violent explosion recorded in modern history, Krakatoa pulverized itself. The eruption lasted two days, and the sound was eventually heard over 2,900 miles away. Some 300 towns were flooded by tidal waves and over 36,000 people killed. Fine dust encircled the earth and remained in the atmosphere for two years, creating magnificent sunsets. From the old caldera beneath the sea, into which the shell of mighty Krakatoa sank, rose Anak Krakatoa—"Child of Krakatoa"—a new island, indeed the child of the same force that destroyed the parent.

More recently, Siberia's Mount Bezymianny expelled 2.4 billion tons of rock in March, 1956. Located in a sparsely inhabited part of the world, it affected few people and made little news.

Across the world, volcanism built a new island under the watchful eyes of science. In late 1963 the island of Surtsey was born in the Atlantic Ocean near Iceland.

And near the village of Paricutin, 200 miles west of Mexico City, farmers watched as a new volcanic cone rose from a small opening in a cornfield. In a week the cone had risen to 500 feet, and five months later it was 1,200 feet above the surrounding land. For nine years, from 1943 through 1952, Mount Paricutin continued its building. In the process a lava flow buried a nearby town.

A discussion of other volcanoes would not be complete without mention of North America's Lassen Peak. Southernmost peak in the Cascades, until the Mount St. Helens eruption, it was the contiguous states' most recent active volcano. From 1914 through 1921, Lassen Peak frequently pelted the neighborhood with ash and itself with lava in an incredible number of *observed* eruptions. No one knows how many minor steam and ash explosions occurred, since the weather in this region, being what it is during the winter, caused the mountain to be obscured and such activity was never recorded. A major, lateral blast, in many ways similar to Mount St. Helens', if not as violent, took place on May 22, 1915. After 65 years the "Devastated Area" still shows the effects of that major eruption.

Mount St. Helens

The Past

The high peaks of the Cascade Range in Washington, Oregon, and northern California are all of volcanic origin. Including British Columbia's Mount Garibaldi, there are 17 snow-capped mountains known to be volcanoes in this chain—all recognized as dormant rather than extinct. That is to say—any *could* become active again. But while there is evidence of current volcanic activity on most of these mountains, it was Mount St. Helens that caught the attention of geologists as the Cascade peak most likely to erupt again soon.

The composite cone, which forms Mount St. Helens today, may be only 1,000 years old. It is an accumulation of successive deposits of ash and lava—the products of regular volcanic activity. This youthful peak sits astride the remains of a much older ancestor, whose age is gauged to be at least 35,000 years. That ancient volcano seems to have been extremely volatile. The products of its eruptions have been identified hundreds of miles away. One of these products is pumice, which emerges during an eruption as frothy lava filled with gas bubbles and hardens quickly around the bubbles—somewhat like a rock of Swiss cheese. St. Helens was sometimes called the place where rocks float, because of the extensive accumulations of pumice. In fact, some pumice does float because it is so thoroughly laced with bubbles that it is lighter than water.

During the early days of the present mountain, some 2,000 years ago before the cone began to form, streams of ropy lava called pahoehoe flowed from a vent on the south side and hardened quickly, leaving tunnels in the flow—the lava caves for which St. Helens is known.

The several Indian tribes that lived in the St. Helens region called the mountain, variously, "Lady of Fire," "Person From Whom Smoke Comes," "Fire Mountain," or some other name referring to smoke and fire. She figured in their legends as an old witch who had been transformed into a raving beauty, or as a woman angry with her two lovers, Mount Hood and Mount Adams. She kept the sacred fire, and the people came from all directions to borrow it.

Captain George Vancouver named the peak Mount St. Helens on May 19, 1792, in honor of Alleyne Fitzherbert, the Baron St. Helens, who had recently executed an important treaty with Spain.

Early settlers in Washington and Oregon posted many accounts of Mount St. Helens' activity during the 1800s. Geologists cannot entirely reconcile reported dates with geologic evidence, but it seems that a period of activity commenced in approximately 1832, built to a rather large eruption in 1842, and then diminished until all activity ceased in 1857. During the 1842 eruption, a French-Canadian voyageur reported that the light was so bright he could see to pick up a pin at midnight.

By 1980 the scars left from the eruptions of the 1800s had healed over, and the young mountain reigned over the southern Washington Cascades with queenly elegance. St. Helens wore a raiment of pristine snow the year round. Her upper slopes were cluttered with pumice rubble in contrast to the rambling meadows found on many other alpine peaks. In her forests, life was abundant.

Herds of Roosevelt Elk and blacktailed deer, the elusive bobcat and cougar, charming raccoons and lumbering black bear made their homes on the ridges and in the valleys. Her lakes and rivers were rich with fish—the Toutle River was said to be one of the finest salmon and steelhead tributaries in the country.

Spirit Lake was kidney-shaped, trapped behind a dam formed of mudslides from past eruptions. Sunk in a glacial depression, it was a young lake whose water had immersed giant Douglas firs. When the wind howled down the canyon and through the trees, it moaned. Perhaps that eerie sound contributed to the Indian belief that spirits inhabited the lake waters.

Bounded by tall firs in the clear, high-country air, the lake, and its environs, was a delightful destination of hundreds of campers and backpackers. Three major youth organizations maintained camps at the lake, and there were four developed public campgrounds to serve the thousands of northwesterners and tourists from around the world who visited the exquisite lake and intriguing mountain. Radiating from Spirit Lake, an extensive trail system penetrated the back country and provided access to several small, high lakes. Spring brought a profusion of wildflowers; summer a restful respite from civilization's hustle and bustle; and in the brisk autumn, hunters trudged the hills and dales seeking game. The winter snowpack attracted cross-country skiers and only the hardiest of downhillers, for there was no developed ski area at Mount St. Helens.

Climbers sought her slopes at all times of the year, for the climb, while not difficult, was exhilarating. And the view from the summit was worth the effort—Mount Rainier and Mount Baker to the north, Mount Adams to the east; Mount Hood, the Sisters and Jefferson in the south.

Mount St. Helens was the crown jewel of the Gifford Pinchot National Forest, even though the very top of her summit was owned by the Burlington Northern Railroad.

And, some people believe, in her remote valleys lived the legendary Sasquatch, or Bigfoot.

Prelude

Earthquakes are a fairly common occurrence where two plates of the earth's crust meet. So the one that was recorded at 3:47 p.m. on March 20, 1980 was not necessarily of particular note, other than it was centered near Mount St. Helens.

But volcanologists had been studying this mountain, and in 1975 they had predicted that it would erupt sometime within a century—maybe even before the end of this one. So when additional earthquakes occurred, the scientists were intrigued. Perhaps the quakes presaged volcanic activity. But they hesitated to make too much of it. The public is not fond of false alarms.

They did not have to postpone a decision long. Just a week later on March 27, shortly after noon, an airborne radio newsman gave the first notice that Mount St. Helens was erupting. In a brief puff, the mountain sent up the first in a series of ash and steam eruptions.

When that eruption was over, there was a new crater carved through the blanket of ice at the mountain's summit and into the rock beneath. It was about the size of a football field and roughly 100 feet deep. A light coating of ash blackened the snow around the crater.

Succeeding ash and steam eruptions created a second crater about 30 feet from the first one, then merged the two into a yawning chasm.

Geologists explained these initial eruptions amounted to the mountain clearing its throat. In the 123 years since previous volcanic activity, ice and rock had fallen into the conduit and plugged it up. Pressure in the magma below the mountain was seeking release. That first ash was simply old rock, pulverized by the force which blasted it out; the steam was simply ground water heated by rising temperatures in the vent. While there was a possibility of a lava eruption, geologists would not go so far as to say there *would* be one. In fact, in the early days of the first eruptions, the major concern was mudslides. Mount St. Helens had several glaciers and a winter snow pack. Volcanic heat could cause the snow and glaciers to melt rapidly and cause avalanches and mudslides.

Officials, without specific guidance from science, opted for caution. In early April a restricted zone was imposed around the peak and no one without specific authorization was permitted to be within that zone. In fact, the restriction was hard to enforce. The whole area was crisscrossed by logging roads and a lot of people who lived there were intimately familiar with the network. Since it was physically impossible to barricade every road, it was impossible to keep everyone out of the area.

It was not surprising that on at least two occasions the adventuresome climbed the heaving peak. On April 3 a solitary climber reached the top. He reported a strong sulphur odor and ash ten feet deep at the edge of the crater. A party of three had just made the summit early in the morning of April 13 when a steam and ash eruption, lasting approximately 20 minutes, bubbled up. They were fortunate that the wind carried the eruption away from them.

A week after that first eruption another phenomenon occurred—harmonic tremors. A harmonic tremor is different kind of earthquake. The usual earthquake causes a sudden sharp jolt and fractures rock. By contrast, harmonic tremors are more like waves in the earth's surface and can be likened to a vibrato. Some people say the best way to visualize a tremor is to imagine the earth's crust as a bowl of shaking gelatin. The tremors, said the scientists, were most likely evidence that magma was moving beneath Mount St. Helens.

And then there was the bulge. Early in April it was noted that the north face of the mountain was bulging out. That bulge eventually reached out about 500 feet from its starting point, having increased at the incredible rate of five feet a day in early May. That, said the geologists, might be caused by magma welling up inside the mountain—but again, no one was sure. But as the bulge increased, it seemed only a matter of time until it broke off in a massive slide. And that was a clear and imminent danger—not to be challenged.

Meanwhile, the people who lived near Mount St. Helens found the novelty of a real, live volcano in the backyard wearing off and the assorted inconveniences imposed by the situation became more noticeable. Particularly affected were the loggers who could not go to work. People who had property in the restricted area could not go to it, and a few who had businesses in the red zone had to close them. Teams of geologists set up instruments to measure any changes, no matter how minute, and scientists and the press swarmed over the mountain recording and reporting its every burp.

An air of expectancy hung over the small communities around Mount St. Helens, but no one knew what to expect or when to expect it.

The people who had homes at or on the way to Spirit Lake became restless. The scouts had already managed to get much of the gear our of their camps, and the homeowners wanted to do the same. The world was captivated by the 84-year-old man who refused to leave his lodge, saying his mountain would never harm him. He received a special dispensation from the $500 fine assessed against anyone found in the red zone who wasn't supposed to be there.

Some people sloughed off warnings of danger. It somehow seemed inconceivable that anything approaching the kind of disaster some scientists said *could* happen ever would. Others, more cautious, did what was feasible to heed warnings as they were issued, placing faith in science and its practitioners to interpret the mountain's unusual behavior.

As April waned, eruptive activity waned, although quakes and tremors continued. In early May, after 16 relatively "quiet" days, a quake measured at 5.0 on the Richter scale shook the mountain, and soon the steam and ash eruptions began anew. The once white slopes of the peak were draped in grey ash, and at the summit there was a massive crater.

The restless Spirit Lake area property owners petitioned the governor for permission to enter the red zone. The harried official finally relented, and on May 17, escorted by police, a caravan of property owners drove to the lake. They had four hours in the red zone and a promise of four more hours the next day. No one was permitted to stay overnight.

May 18, 1980

May 18 dawned clear and calm. Nothing exceptional was going on to give note that a major eruption was in sight. No larger than usual quakes occurred. No preliminary bursts of steam. No slipping and sliding of the monstrous bulge. No auxiliary shots of debris. No lava. No rise in temperature.

A dedicated geologist, camped some five miles north of the peak, reported to his base in Vancouver that nothing was new.

Up in the Green River valley, over 15 miles north and a few ridges away, some campers were getting up to start their breakfast.

Two geologists and their pilot were flying over the mountain in a small plane. It was a thrilling experience—their first close look at a subject dear to them. They probably hoped the mountain would do something for them.

It did.

That pilot may have been the first person to give notice to the world of the incredible explosion that wracked the mountain. He reported to Air Traffic Control that the whole north side of the mountain "just went."

At 8:31 a.m. a quake shook the mountain. The bulge on the north face slid away and out of the open rolled a cloud of ash and steam. Right behind that came tremendously hot gasses, the incredible pressure trapped in the magma chamber below the mountain was finally released, to explode like the granddaddy of all pressure cookers.

This practically instantaneous release of enormous pressure created a shock wave that surged down valleys and up over ridges carrying ash, steam, mud, and rock. The wind reached hurricane force—almost 200 miles an hour.

By May 18th, the St. Helens' eruptions must have been routine to the air traffic controllers. They asked the pilot if he could give an estimate of how much of the mountain was gone, then asked him for verification when he told them, "the whole side."

The explosion made a loud bang heard as far away as Vancouver, British Columbia, Canada, 225 miles north. It continued all day in successive billows of purple-blue clouds, which look in photos like so much purple cauliflower.

Within ten minutes commercial pilots in the air near the billowing cloud reported that they couldn't accurately estimate the breadth and height of the plume. It was described by the usually laconic pilots as incredible, spectacular. They told Air Traffic Control that they were seeing a great deal of lightning.

Responsible agencies scrambled to get observers in the air and rescue equipment on the ground. By early afternoon Army helicopters were flying low over the Toutle River Valley, searching for survivors. Unable to see through the clouds to know just what was occurring on the mountain, pilots and their crews risked their lives to rescue several stranded people—and to give word to the world of the enormity of what had happened. The chopper crews alerted the state patrol to the wall of mud surging down the Toutle Valley, and probably many lives were saved because it was possible to evacuate threatened people in time.

Those animals still alive stood stunned and in shock. A cataclysm had occurred that would profoundly affect the lives of hundreds of people and hundreds of thousands of other living things.

Mere numbers—dollars, statistics, hours, weeks, and years—cannot tell the story. The story is in the people and their land, and how both will never be the same again.

The Survivors

The little dramas of life are the big stories of people caught in events not of their own making. Thiry-one people are known to have died in the May 18 eruption; another 34 are still unaccounted for. But there were some people in the Mount St. Helens area that morning for whom the clock had not yet run out.

An elderly man and his four dogs sat out the inferno in their cabin ten miles southwest of the blast. They were flown out 13 days later unharmed.

A party of six, two women, two men, and two teenage boys were camped on a ridge north of the cone, five miles out of the red zone. At the first puffs of the fatal explosion they were delighted. They had a perfect view through the saddle of an intervening ridge. Then they saw the massive explosion. At first it looked like a baseball, then it broadened out. The mountain disappeared as they watched. Then they heard a roaring sound, which got louder and louder. They could see trees being uprooted as the force of the blast raced toward them. It took the shock wave less than a minute to reach them.

At that point they scrambled into one of their two vehicles, abandoned a pickup truck, all the camping equipment, and some clothing. At speeds up to 60 miles per hour, they raced the car down the narrow, winding logging road. One of the six people remembers feeling the heat on the back of his neck. On the way they saw other campers, blissfully unaware of the hell that was about to engulf them. Hurricane-force winds caught up with the speeding, bouncing car, and the sky darkened. Heat lightning added to the netherworld scenario. The fact that the road crossed a logged out area probably saved the car from being smashed under falling trees. As they neared the paved road, blobs of mud coated the car. Finally, at the highway the mud gave way to ash, and they sped to safety.

Southward, a young couple was camped by the Toutle River. The water rose so fast that they climbed to the top of their car to escape. The car was knocked loose, and the frightened pair was dumped into a swirling maelstrom of logs. Almost trapped among the churning wood, the two scrambled out. Rescuers waded through mud up to their chests in order to reach the pair.

Six campers, 30 air miles from the mountain, awoke to find trees toppling about them. With no warning, two of them found themselves buried in ash and timber. They couldn't see and didn't know what was happening. Frantically digging and clawing, it took them ten minutes to hew their way to an embattled world under night-black sky. Of the four friends who were with them, two were not to be

seen again. Leaving two badly injured friends in a shack, the man and woman began, what was to be, a 15-mile hike to safety. A helicopter returned to ferry out the injured.

Three loggers were working in the blast zone. Burned over large parts of their bodies by hot ash and cinders, two of them hiked eight miles through choking dust, in miserable pain, before being found.

Elsewhere, a young family, parents and two daughters, one aged four and the other an infant, had backpacked to a campsite along the Green River trail. The woman remembers a low rumbling, then rapid air pressure changes that made their ears pop repeatedly. The sky turned black, as ash began to bury the campsite. No fast escape could be attempted with two small children, so the family found refuge in an abandoned shack. It was small protection from the holocaust, but it provided shelter from the rain of debris.

That night the family stayed in their tent, and in the morning sought to reach their car. Trails had been obliterated in the dust and fallen trees blocked the way. The four lived on survival food, carried in their backpacks, and were thankful for a small spring where they could get fresh water.

By noon they became worried. How would they get out? A rescue chopper buzzing overhead seemed unaware that they were there. But the pilot did spot them, and was astonished to see people alive on the dead land. He was unable to land right at that area, but sent rescuers in on foot to escort the survivors to a safer landing spot.

And the pair of geologists and their pilot, delightedly snapping pictures on several passes around the mountain, may well be the last people alive today to have seen Spirit Lake. Air Traffic Control asked the pilot if he would like to turn back to take another look. ''Negative,'' he replied. Diving to increase airspeed, the little craft sped south to safety. Those aboard it had missed destruction by less than a second.

The fate of many of the people who are unaccounted for may never be known. One of them is the 84-year-old man who refused to leave his beloved mountain. Where he and his cats had made their home is now covered with tons of mud.

And the last that is known of the intense, young geologist is his final call, an excited, not frightened, ''Vancouver, Vancouver, this is it!''

The Shattered Land

Where once the rolling hills and ridges were carpeted with fir forests, there is now a barren wasteland. Where once clear mountain streams gurgled over eroded pebbles, there is mud. Where once loggers worked the forests, they now attempt to clear away enough debris to reach the billion board feet of downed timber, some of which may be salvageable.

Where once there were homes in which people lived and vacationed, there are now shells of buildings ripped from their foundations and deposited askew in the mud. Where there was a two-lane highway to Spirit Lake, there is now rubble.

And 1,277 feet of the top of the mountain is gone. Where there used to be a graceful snow-covered cone, there is a squat black butte. Someone commented that the mountain looks as though a third of its top had been neatly sliced off with a giant cleaver.

A huge crater is left—shaped like a giant amphitheater, it measures a mile by two miles and is 3,000 feet deep, open to the north.

Cities in the path of the ash cloud were left with the challenge of how to get rid of tons of ash, which covered them like snow.

Eastern Washington is an important agricultural area. Volcanic ash deposits, eventually, become rich, fertile land for crops. But ash deposited on the crops themselves is something else. There is no body of scientific study to aid the farmers in dealing with effects of ash, so the net effect of the blanket of ash cast upon young crops cannot even be predicted. What happens to the equipment used to plant, nurture, and harvest those crops is easily learned. The abrasive ash works on metal like sandpaper on wood. Farmers face the peril of bringing the crops to maturity despite the ash, then being unable to harvest them because of the danger of ruining expensive equipment.

Thirty-three ships were at dock at the several ports above the confluence of the Cowlitz and Columbia rivers, where the ship channel was most seriously clogged with ash and debris. Some of them were unable to leave the harbors for several weeks. Others waited far down the Columbia until the river was dredged sufficiently so they could pass.

It could take an army of statisticians years to assess the damage—which cannot be entirely measured in statistics anyway. How does one put a dollar value on the swallows that starved to death because ash had killed off all the insects on which they feed?

Is there any way to measure the inconveniences imposed on almost everyone who lives and works anywhere near Mount St. Helens?

Where once a river teemed with fish, there is barely a river left. The glacial ice, which fed it, has all melted. How does one measure the hours and minutes of fishing in a favorite spot, never more to be had. What, if anything, can be done for animals who have lost their homes?

In truth the effects of Mount St. Helens' eruption will continue to be felt in many ways for a long, long, time.

Postlude

What does a mountain do for an encore? If it is Mount St. Helens, it goes right on erupting, albeit with not quite so much enthusiasm.

Less than two weeks after the huge May 18 eruption, on May 25, a new cloud of steam and ash was emitted. This second eruption sent a cloud to 20,000 feet, and cities to the south and west got their first taste of volcanic ash. That very light dusting had hardly been swept up when, on June 12, late in the evening, Mount St. Helens went off again. People in southwest Washington and northwest Oregon awoke on Friday, June 13, to their first real taste of more than just a little bit of ash. While the total accumulation probably did not exceed 1/16 of an inch, the Oregonians could now feel sympathy for the plight of their less fortunate neighbors in Washington, still trying to get rid of the May 18 ash.

Meanwhile, during the first few days after the May 18 explosion, the battered properties along the Toutle faced a new threat. A 200-foot-high, 17-mile-long earthen dam had been emplaced at the outlet of Spirit Lake. Water quickly rose behind it, and geologists feared the dam would not hold. Residents were allowed to visit their homes for very brief periods under the watchful escort of law enforcement personnel. Within a week the water level dropped. Apparently the dam would hold.

Regardless of the risk, scientists flocked to the devastated area to look and learn. They found a dead land. Portions of the area around Spirit Lake were buried under as much as 400 feet of ash. On May 22 the water temperature in the lake was 92 degrees Fahrenheit; on June 1 the lake measured from 75 to 100 feet deep, and the temperature had risen to 97 degrees on the surface, and 95 degrees at the very bottom.

Harried geologists, sated with new data to chew on, still could not predict what the mountain would do next, let alone when. They did predict that a lava dome would build in the crater, since in the past, this was a customary aftermath of this kind of eruption. The continually cloudy weather made visual observation spotty, but radar imagery presented continuing coverage of what was happening in the crater.

On May 30 the mountain fulfilled the prediction. A lava dome was beginning to build on top of the vent. What was happening, said the scientists, was that lava was welling up through the conduit and solidifying when chilled by the cold air. As more lava was extruded, it would push up from beneath, building the dome from the bottom. Observers looked in vain for a red glow, evidence of lava running into the crater from under the dome.

Periodic puffs of steam and ash continued as did harmonic tremors and earthquakes. Heavy clouds blanketed the area, making visual observation difficult, but the volcano's activities were monitored both by radar and high-flying, specially equipped aircraft.

So many scientists, reporters, and photographers sought entrance to the endangered area that a committee was appointed to screen these requests. Each party to enter the area would be required to maintain radio contact at all times, and no member was to travel further than a 15-minute hike from the vehicle.

The dome kept growing. On June 21 it was more than 200 feet high and over 600 feet wide. A week later it was astonishing the scientists, growing 80 feet a day. All over the floor of the massive crater were hundreds of fumaroles. A cloud of steam hung over the mountain almost all the time. The air above it reeked with sulphur. News stories reported that anywhere from 50 to 1,300 tons of sulfur dioxide were being emitted from the mountain.

Geologists became concerned that the dome was plugging the vent, which would allow pressure to build again and precipitate another eruption. They were right. On July 22 pressure shattered the lava dome, sending its fragments flying and an ash cloud 11 miles up. It was the second largest eruption and was followed in quick succession by two more major and three minor eruptions before the evening was over. Ash again drifted east, dusting the same beleaguered Washington communities again. This eruption was estimated at around 700 feet in diameter. Glowing rocks were visible within the new crater, and this, it was said, indicated the temperature within the vent could be as much as 13,000 degrees Fahrenheit.

On August 7 Mount St. Helens erupted again. There was a cloud sent up to over 44,000 feet and a pyroclastic flow. But this time scientists said they may have determined how to predict it. They said the nature of preceding quakes, harmonic tremors, and ratio of gasses being vented have established an identifiable pattern. Four hours before the blast, an alert was sounded. All loggers working in the area, scientists, reporters, and residents were given ample warning to evacuate.

As summer wanes and autumn rains become imminent, builders work against time to construct earthen walls to retain the mass of debris in the Toutle Valley. The rain is expected to run off the compacted, cement-like ash very quickly and create massive flooding conditions.

If Mount St. Helens remains true to its past patterns of eruptive activity, northwesterners can expect a long siege. The last period of volcanic activity lasted 15 years. With the novelty beginning to wear off, people in the area feel a little weary of the volcano and its antics. What it has done and what it will do will determine much of the way of life of its people, who are learning to live with a volcano.

Epilogue

In an instant a swatch of land reaching 15 miles from the center of the blast, some of western United States' most lovely mountain countryside, was transformed. Today it is the land of Hades brought to life—in death.

It will never again be what we remember in our lifetime, or in the lifetimes of many generations of our descendants. The Mount St. Helens that our great-great grandchildren will know will be vastly different than it was before or is today. Here we have a volcanic showcase, a living laboratory where man can observe what happens to the land after it has been wiped clean and nature starts over.

Seeing is believing—but do you really want to see it? You want to remember it as it was, the captivating Spirit Lake, the invigorating climb to Norway Pass, the mists on the trails in the back country, the little lakes nestled in granite depressions. The Plains of Abraham, worth every huff and puff to get there for cross-country skiing. The mystery of Bigfoot. The crater filled with sparkling snow, blushing in the early morning sun at the end of the daybreak climb.

The view of Mount Rainier, rising majestically in the north, the lodges and campgrounds and trails and trees and flowers. A mountain with a mystique.

It's all gone.

The curious will flock to see and be awed. Scientists from around the world will come to study the havoc wrought and, as the years pass, the exciting birth and development of a new biological community on the virgin land.

The eruption, and what it did, is the basis of which legends will be born. It is our reminder that man cannot control nature. He never has and probably never will—and perhaps should not want to.

Mount St. Helens, 1980—an end—and a beginning.

The Cascades, Volcano Wonderland

The young, quixotic Cascades are so called because Lewis and Clark, in traversing the Columbia Gorge, referred to the mountains that tower over it as "the mountains by the Cascades." The name stuck.

The peace a harried city dweller finds in these rugged outlands is both real and misleading. For these are mountains born and shaped by violence—young mountains, as mountains go. The oldest of peaks dates back seven million years, just a wink in geological time.

To appreciate how it is that each of the 17 major volcanoes in the Cascade range can be so different from each of the others, when they all had the same origin, it is necessary to understand some of the things that happen in the mountain building process. First of all, not everything that comes out of a volcano is lava. There is steam, assorted volcanic gasses, and debris left over from previous eruptions as well as lava. In fact, all lava is not alike. The viscosity—how fluid it is—makes a big difference. Thin lava does not trap a great deal of gas, the motive power of the volcanic eruption, thus, this lava tends not to erupt violently. Regardless of viscosity, lava is also classified by the amount of silica it contains. This too has a great deal to do with how lava behaves.

Lava may erupt in huge, fiery fountains, and the particles solidify before they hit the ground. If the lava is frothy and has a high silica content, it winds up as pumice, a sort of rock Swiss cheese. A general term for other fragmented lava is tephra, or pyroclastics—literally, fire-broken pieces. A pyroclastic flow occurs when fragmented material, often ash, is suspended in hot gas that flows away from the eruption site.

Lava may flow away from the vent, or opening, in the volcano and leave thick sheets of rock, or it may rise to the top of the vent and simply form a lava dome. Such a dome may grow to hundreds of feet in height as new lava pushes up from underneath. The lava in the vent may solidify, forming a lava plug.

Centuries of erosion wearing away at the surrounding mountain may eventually expose the lava plug. Such plugs are steep, interesting formations that in some places stand alone as monolithic rocks on otherwise flat plains.

Most of the major Cascade volcanoes are stratovolcanoes, or composite volcanoes. That is, they are built of successive layers of lava flows and fragmented materials. Some are cinder cones—composed entirely of pyroclastics; or shield domes—built entirely of lava flows; or plug domes—one huge, solid lava dome.

If Americans had not thought much about volcanoes before, Mount St. Helens' antics have made them rapidly, and in some cases painfully, aware that their lovely Northwest mountains are volcanoes. This, of course, has been known by geologists and other interested people all along.

But geology may seem to be a study of "lifeless" things—rocks and dirt—and, as such, not very interesting. So, suddenly, geology became to northwesterners a highly personal thing. The geologists are the interpreters of the remarkable chain of events that have changed southwestern Washington's landscape and affected the lives of everyone in the area. What can they tell us about the other volcanoes of the Cascades? How were they built? What has happened to them and because of them? And what will they do in the future?

Every mountain has its own unique character—a composite of its structure, its surroundings, its climate, its wildlife and its place in the lives of men who live and play at its feet. Those of the Cascades are no different. Each has its story.

Mount Rainier

Massive, yet only partially the size it once was, Mount Rainier dominates the skyline in northwestern Washington state. It is the city of Tacoma's own mountain, but it is also visible from Seattle, Everett, Olympia, Bellingham, and even as far south as Portland, Oregon. This massif, at 14,410 feet the highest peak in Washington and second highest in the lower 48 states, is a bit of the Arctic, over 1,300 miles south of the real place.

Built of the leavings of volcanism, Mount Rainier has been sculptured into a breathtaking, scenic wonderland by the greatest collection of glaciers located on one mountain in North America, outside of Alaska. Canyons sweep from the bases of its glaciers, funneling melt water down valleys and creating several rivers.

Mount Rainier juts so far above its surroundings that it generates its own weather system. On the western flanks, it gathers moisture-laden clouds from the Pacific Ocean and

Mt. St. Helens was a popular winter recreation area. The north
side, seen here, was blown out in the May 18 eruption.
(Following pages) Early January sunset bathes Mt. St. Helens' regal
peak in warm pink. This view is from the northwest.

Mt. St. Helens' ice cream cone summit framed in the greenery
of Portland's Rose Test Gardens.

In the fall sunrise, the photographer's telephoto lens enlarges Mt. St. Helens as seen overlooking downtown Portland.

An early steam eruption sends a small plume from the summit. Yale Lake, south of Mt. St. Helens, is in the foreground.

Two ''small'' craters have almost completely merged into one large pit in early April, 1980. Note the snow around the summit is grey with coating of ash.

Mt. St. Helens' first eruption, March 27, 1980, left an ash-blackened dimple in the snow at the mountain's summit.

25

Turbulent winds in and over the mile-wide, 1,300 foot deep crater made helicopter observations of Mt. St. Helens, such as this one in late April, risky.

Deceivingly serene, Mt. St. Helens sports light issue of steam May 17.
(Following page) At 8:31 a.m., May 18, 1980, the north face of Mt. St. Helens
slid away, and massive eruption sheared off the cone-shaped summit. Purple
cauliflower clouds of steam and ash continued to billow skyward throughout the day.
Compare this view from Yale Lake with pages 17 (before) and 33 (after).

No man's land of bleak devastation in northward path of May 18 blast on Mt. St. Helens. Timber was toppled or uprooted, and the entire land shorn of vegetation up to 15 miles from blast center.
(Preceeding page) Late in the day, May 18, 1980, the day of the big eruption.

Denuded hills, the "new" Spirit Lake, and a blackened mountain. Gone is St. Helens symmetrical, cone-shaped summit. In its place is the yawning, amphitheater-shaped crater large enough to hold a small airport.

Twelve miles north of the summit, folded mountain terrain on Mt. St. Helens is grey in death.

Ground water continues to seep toward hot lava rising in volcanic conduit, to be vaporized and rise as a steam plume from the crater. Compare this "after" view from Yale Lake with pages 17 and 28.

Gaping crater in bare mountain with steam wafting from volcanic vent could easily be a scene from a science fiction movie.

A few tree trunks, stripped of limbs, still stand near a border of blast-devastated area. June 30, 1980.

The extent of devastation north of the peak can be seen in this view looking south, with Mt. Hood rising over the Columbia River, far left.

One billion board feet of timber was damaged or destroyed during the May 18 eruption. Some of it may be salvageable if logging equipment can be gotten into the area to work it.

*Steam rises from a new crater within the crater, July 29, 1980, a week after the
second largest of five major eruptions shattered the lava dome. Sunset
burnishes the crater rim, and leaves the floor in a shadow.
(Following pages) From West Point, south of Mt. St. Helens, late in the day
May 18. Throughout the day, subsidiary eruptions continued to pump
steam and ash skyward and the cloud drifted north and east.*

"New" Spirit Lake retains its kidney shape. The water is partially covered with debris. Small craters created by "rootless" vents can be seen on the lake's south shore (center). These "rootless" vents occur where water is heated to steam in mud beneath surface and erupts in miniature geysers.

A massive mudflow surged west down the Toutle River on May 18. Maximum height of flow can be seen on tree trunk over 30 miles from peak, near Interstate Highway 5.

That pile of ''toothpicks'' is an accumulation of downed timber on the south side of Spirit Lake. Pock-mark craters left by steam eruptions from ''rootless'' vents leave the land with a lunar-like appearance.

July 29, 1980—The first rays of the morning sun bathe Mt. St. Helens in a pinkish hue as the moon looks on.

44

*Small band of timber, protected by intervening ridge, is left standing in the midst
of devastated hills. Mt. Rainier presides in the background.
Note page 47, taken from the same vantage point.*

Mt. St. Helens now has the silhouette of a broad, flat-topped mesa. The photographer turned the camera from northward view on page 46 to look east here. June 30, 1980.

Mt. Adams, east of St. Helens, peaks through evening mist.
July 29, 1980.

July 22, 1980 eruption of Mt. St. Helens, seen from Oregon.
Mt. Rainier is in the background.

49

Observers in a small plane view lava dome forming on the crater floor. The dome was as big as Seattle's King Dome stadium before the July 22 eruption shattered it.

Lava dome formed at the top of volcanic vent in floor of crater. The lava seeping to the surface solidified on contact with the cold air. More lava pushed up beneath, cracking the gap. In late evening, as daylight diminished, red-hot lava can be seen in the new cracks.

Floor of crater lies approximately 3,000 feet below the south wall rim.
The crater is two miles long, a mile wide.

The blackened, flat-topped south face of Mt. St. Helens, the volcano's "back."

Cloud cover at approximately 7,000 feet nestles on crater floor. A plume of steam hangs suspended in sunset light. June 17, 1980.

Spot of blue (right center) is Spirit Lake. Volcano was dozing
peacefully in this July 27, 1980 photo.

*July 2, 1980. Some greenery flourishes on the edge of the
devastated area west of Mt. St. Helens.*

Route of May 18 pyroclastic flow can be seen in broad sloping sweep away from the north side of the crater. From northeast of the mountain at sunset, July 29, 1980.

Veil of steam drifts in crater. Note new "small" crater left by July 22 eruption.

Rock at top of vent is heated to red hot by lava welling up from below.
Sunset glow bathes eastern crater wall in pink and purple.

July 22 eruption at sunset. Three major eruptions occurred within a few hours.

Red-hot rock in the new crater glows through a veil of steam.

July 22 eruption shoots above Mt. St. Helens. Photo taken from the south, with Mt. Rainier behind.

Residents of Portland, Oregon, 45 miles south of Mt. St. Helens, had a good view of the July 22 eruption.
(Following page) The brooding volcano on Portland's northern skyline.

*Mt. Garibaldi, 40 miles north of Vancouver, British Columbia,
is 8,787 feet in elevation.*

*Mt. Adams, 33 miles due east of Mt. St. Helens, is the second highest
mountain in the Pacific Northwest at 12,286 feet.
(Preceeding page) Mt. St. Helens from Yale Lake, September 15, 1980.*

Mt. Shasta, located approximately 40 miles south of the California-Oregon border in northwest California, dominates the surrounding Cascade landscape.

Crater Lake, in southern Oregon, was once Mt. Mazama and had an elevation of over 12,000 feet before its cataclysmic eruption approximately 6,600 years ago.

Mt. Washington, between Bend, Oregon and Eugene, Oregon, is one of the oldest of the volcanoes in the western United States.
(Following pages) Mt. Rainier, with an elevation of 14,410 feet, is the highest mountain in the state of Washington.

Mt. Baker, in north-central Washington, has an elevation of 10,778 feet.

Mt. Hood, at 11,245 feet, is located 40 miles east of Portland. Note the
steam rising from "hot spots" on the mountain in this picture, taken in 1974.

Mt. Adams, named after President Adams, occasionally emits steam and
other gases, which are visible from summit crevices.
(Following pages) Crater Lake, formed from a cataclysmic volcanic explosion, left
a six mile wide basin now filled with water almost 4,000 feet deep. This is
one of the true scenic wonders of the world.

Mt. Rainier, visible from both Canada and the state of Oregon, presents a different profile from each side viewed.

The surrounding area of Mt. Hood abounds in natural scenic beauty.

Mt. Rainier, approximately 60 miles south of Seattle,
last erupted between 1820 and 1854.

Timberline Lodge stands at 6,000 feet on Mt. Hood's south side.

Mt. Lassen, with an elevation of 10,457 feet, is one of the youngest of the
Cascade volcanoes, coming into being about 11,000 years ago.
(Following pages) Mt. Hood, with an elevation of 11,245 feet, is known as
one of the most beautiful mountains in the world. It last experienced
volcanic eruptions between 1846 and 1865.

A view of Mt. Hood from Devil's Peak.

*Mt. Shasta, at 14,161 feet above sea level, can be seen
from a distance of over 200 miles.
(Following pages) Left to right: Mt. Washington, Three Fingered Jack and
Mt. St. Helens (right above it), Mt. Jefferson, and Mt. Hood as
photographed from the Three Sisters.*

*Mt. Thielsen, one of the oldest of the Cascade volcanoes,
rises above the east shore of Diamond Lake.*

This aerial view of Crater Lake from the south gives the viewer an idea of
the magnitude of the cataclysmic eruption of Mt. Mazama.
(Following pages) Mt. Rainier. Because of its geological restlessness, a volcano
watch is kept at all times by the University of Washington and the U.S. Geological Survey.

Of the famed Three Sisters, the North Sister (10,085 feet) and the Middle
Sister (10,047 feet) as photographed in evening light.

The South Sister, standing at 10,358 feet, is one of the famed Three Sister (Faith, Hope, Charity) Mountains in the central Cascades of Oregon.

Mt. Adams, approximately 50 miles south of Mt. Rainier, has no record of eruption in modern times.

Mt. Rainier supports the single largest glacial system in the contiguous 48 states, and is the mother of several northwest rivers.

Mt. Hood, standing at 11,245 feet, is the second most often climbed peak in the world.

Early morning mist rises from Diamond Lake.
Mt. Bailey is in the background.

Mt. St. Helens as photographed from the Pittock Mansion
in Portland, October of 1979.
(Following pages) Geologists today believe that Mt. Hood
once stood 750 feet taller.

Mt. McLoughlin, elevation 11,493 feet, and a prominent landmark in southern Oregon, is approximately 100,000 years old.

Natural scenic beauty in Mt. Hood National Forest.

Broken Top, standing at 9,175 feet in central Oregon, appears to have experienced a similar type eruption to that of the recent Mt. St. Helens explosion, leaving a large semi-circular amphitheatre.

Looking from the north over Mt. Washington, the famed Three Sisters stand majestically clothed in winter's garb.

*Mt. McLoughlin, the highest peak between Shasta and the Three Sisters, was
later renamed for Dr. John McLoughlin
of early Oregon history.
(Following pages) Mt. Baker, left and in the distance, has experienced a
noticeable increase of thermal activity since March of 1975.*

*Mt. Washington, in the central Cascade range, is known to have been
extinct as far back as the Pleistocene age, 1¾ million years ago.*

Mt. Baker was first named the ''Great White Watcher'' in 1790 by Spanish explorer Manuel Quimper. It was later renamed by Captain George Vancouver in 1792 for his third lieutenant, Joseph Baker.

Mt. Jefferson, at 10,495 feet, is the second highest mountain in Oregon. It is named after President Thomas Jefferson.

Mt. Shasta, in northern California, is not a single peak, but a multiple structure of four volcanoes piled on top or against each other.

Mt. Hood as seen from Portland's nationally famous Rose Test Gardens. Mt. Hood is the only mountain in the U.S. to offer year-around skiing.

Mt. Thielsen, at 9,178 feet, with its high spire that attracts lightning
is known as the "Lightning Rod of the Cascades."
(Following pages) The South Sister, with Sparks Lake in the foreground.
The Three Sisters are as likely as any of the western volcanoes
to come back to life.

Mt. Rainier still produces steam eruptions, indicating
continuing thermal activity within the mountain.

Mt. Rainier has been an active volcano for over a million years.

Mt. Bachelor, at 9,065 feet, is also known as Bachelor Butte, and has several "hot spots" on its northern slopes. (Following pages) The early morning sun creates a picturesque view of Mt. Hood, the tallest mountain in the Oregon Cascades.

Mt. Rainier, towering 14,410 feet, is a most conspicuous landmark within a radius of 200 miles. Here it rises above Elliot Bay. (Following pages) The North and Middle Sisters of the famed Three Sisters, as photographed from Scott Lake.

Black Butte, a plug dome at Mt. Shasta's western base, rises 2,500 feet above the surrounding area.

The summit of Mt. Hood. Note the steam and areas of melted snow, caused by "hot spots."

Mt. Hood from Larch Mountain, Oregon.

northern border at that point.

Of all the Cascade peaks, Mount Hood is probably the most developed for recreational use. It has four developed ski areas, some of which are lighted for night skiing. One has the only year-round ski slope in the United States, with a lift to 9,000 feet. Ski racing teams train here and summer skiing is becoming very popular.

There are innumerable campgrounds and sites scattered about Hood, and the Skyline Trail, which circles the peak at approximately the 7,000-foot level, is traversed by hundreds of hikers and backpackers annually.

Probably two reasons Mount Hood is so well used are its accessibility and its proximity to a major population center. Since it is not an especially rugged peak, and much of the surrounding region has been well logged, there is a complex of roads on its slopes. Some are paved, many are Forest Service and logging roads ranging from good gravel surface to trails barely wide enough for one vehicle. In short it is possible to drive to, or within a couple of miles of, almost anywhere on the mountain, outside the wilderness area above the timberline.

Mount Hood's most famous attraction is Timberline Lodge. The beautiful, massive building is at the timberline on the south face. Built as a public works project by the Civilian Conservation Corps in the 1930s, the lodge is constructed of stone and huge hand-hewn logs, with a floor of great stone slabs. The lodge is the starting point for most climbing parties, the warming center for skiers, and the delight of tourists. Next to Fujiyama, Mount Hood is the most often climbed volcanic peak in the world.

When climbers reach Crater Rock, an outcrop of solidified lava, they see present-day evidence of Mount Hood's volcanism. There are several fumeroles, gas vents and other hot spots issuing hot water and steam. Elsewhere in the Hood region are Bagby Hot Springs, where the warm water is a pleasant temperature for bathing.

Like other Cascade volcanoes, Mount Hood is a composite cone, although the original shape has been glaciated, eroded and changed by lava and mudflows. It is believed the original cone grew to a height of several thousand feet in the first ten years of its existence. A few of the original lava flows were 500 feet deep. The mountain continued to grow through millenia, built of ash, rock, and lava of explosive eruptions. During Earth's cool periods, glaciers grew and left their marks, deep-scarred valleys between lava ridges. Mudflows, created when volcanic eruptions melted glaciers, may have reached the Columbia River.

Once the mountain reached its maximum height, eruptions commenced from two new vents that poured lava down the north and northeast sides. During a glacial period about 25,000 years ago, an immense ice sheet almost covered Mount Hood. This massive sheet wore away 1,000 feet from the summit.

About 200 years ago a period of volcanic activity occurred, during which numerous mudflows covered the south and southwest sides of the mountain.

There are extensive writings of Mount Hood's various eruptions during the last century. None, of course, was of the magnitude of St. Helens' enormous 1980 blast, but at least one was observed to "shoot up a column of fire" and produce "hot cinders"—indications of a lava eruption. That eruption, in August of 1859, was seen from Portland, 60 miles west.

A similar eruption occurred in September, 1865, and an observer reported smoke and flames issued from the mountain's summit.

In an unusual incident in 1907, a climbing party noticed a day-long emission of steam from a point near Crater Rock and a red glow at night. Soon afterward the White River, which originates in a nearby glacier, became swollen with so much water that the only reasonable explanation could be a sudden glacial melt from abnormally warm conditions within the mountain.

With Northwest people so aware of volcanoes and their destructive potential, it is no wonder that when a series of quakes was registered near Mount Hood in early July, 1980, people were alarmed. Science kept a close watch, although geologists felt the quakes were not precursors of eruptive activity. By the following week it had been established that at least some of the jolting of seismographs may have originated with tree-stump blasting at the mountain.

In a detailed scenario prepared in 1974, a Portland State University geology professor described what might happen should Mount Hood erupt again. Prophetically, some Toutle River valley dwellers might say, this scenario predicted that most of the damage to man and his property would come from mudflows.

Mount Shasta

As Rainier dominates the central Washington Cascades, so does Shasta loom over the northern California range. Sprawled out on a high plateau, rising 10,000 feet above its base, Shasta's summit is 14,162 feet above sea level. When conditions are right, it can be seen from the Pacific Ocean.

The lonely giant is actually two mountains: Shasta itself, which is the principal peak, and its immediate neighbor Shastina, which, if stood alone would rank as a major mountain in its own right. Shastina is 12,330 feet tall and is the third highest peak in the Cascades, after Shasta and Rainier. And Shasta and Shastina are just the most visible evidence of one of the Cascades' most complex volcanoes. For Mount Shasta is not just one or two, but a compound of four separate volcanoes with many smaller, parasitic vents.

Observers had long been intrigued by the fact that Mount Shasta's south side, exposed to more sunlight, showed evidence of greater glacial erosion than the north and east sides, where such erosion would be expected to happen. But now it is known that the south side is what is left of the oldest of the four cones. Adjacent to the eroded ridge, which is all that is left of that early volcano, is a newer cone called Misery Hill by climbers who toil up its sides. Shastina and the present summit developed within the last 10 to 12 thousand years.

Just west of the mountain's base is Black Butte, a conical dome that appears to be a cylinder cone, but isn't. Rather it is a plug dome, built from one continuous extrusion of lava, probably about 10,000 years ago. The period of explosive activity, during which these latest volcanic features were born, must have been one of great violence. There is evidence of extensive mudflows and large pyroclastic flows.

More recently, another vent opened and issued thick lava flows that created Hotlum cone, the site of one of Shasta's five glaciers.

Since man has been observing Shasta, there has been no notable volcanic activity. In the 1850s it was reported that a few puffs of smoke were issued from the crater, but no steam and ash eruptions have been proven. However, a climbing party noted boiling hot springs in the summit crater, more extensive than the one small spring there today.

East of Mount Shasta is evidence of another kind of volcanism in the Cascades. Dotted with parasitic cones, Medicine Lake Highland is what remains of a collapsed shield volcano. Perhaps more accessible to the curious who want to see what volcanoes do is the nearby Lava Beds National Monument, site of several manifestations of past volcanic performance.

Mount Shasta's air of mystery has attracted a host of cults and believers in the occult. They say it is home to a variety of secretive, or lost peoples, the fabled Lemurians and lost Yaktayvians: little people, big people, and bell users. Believers say that the inside of the mountain is hollow, and at least two of the secretive tribes make their homes within. Other cults contend that Mount Shasta is an interplanetary port of call.

Shasta is a beautiful, regal mountain. It is the source of two of the three rivers that feed Lake Shasta. This huge lake was created by a dam on the Sacramento River and backs up into the valleys of three rivers and dozens of tributary creeks; altogether it has a shoreline that is 370 miles long. The lake and the mountain are prime recreation areas for all of northern California. Each weekend thousands of city-weary people from the San Francisco Bay area make the several hours drive north to rest in the clean, cool environs of a sleeping volcano.

Crater Lake

Perhaps the best example of creation caused by volcanic destruction is Oregon's Crater Lake. It is strikingly beautiful, extremely deep, and vividly blue. With neither an inlet nor an outlet, a balance of accumulation and evaporation keeps the surface of the lake at a steady 1,932 feet above the floor of the caldera in which it lies.

That caldera is the huge crater left after a mountain, now named Mount Mazama, blew its top. This volcano erupted so much material from the magma chamber beneath it, that the remaining shell collapsed into the void, leaving a gaping pit six miles in diameter. In the 6,600 years since that cataclysmic explosion, new lava streamed across the crater floor, sealing the old vent, and the crater filled with water to form the enchanting lake, deepest in North America.

The crater walls rise 500 to 2,000 feet above the lake. Atop the wall a one-way paved road circles the crater, giving the sightseer dozens of remarkable views. High points jutting above the crater rim, The Watchman, Llao Rock, jutting above the crater rim, The Watchman, Llao Rock, and Hillman Peak, are remnants of earlier lava flows.

Crater Lake National Park has a lodge and campgrounds to accommodate visitors. It's advised that even summer visitors should be prepared for frosty nights.

Mount Mazama is one of the most thoroughly studied volcanoes in the Cascades. It was born a few million years ago and grew steadily in a long, continuing series of eruptions that built a broader, more gently sloping mountain than some of the hastily created steep cones. In the process it overran what was left of a previous volcano. It is believed the Phantom Cone, a jagged protuberance in Crater Lake, may be a lava dike from that prehistoric predecessor.

Around the peak, created by that original vent, developed a great number of parasitic cones, which in time all became a part of a vast, complex mountain. Remnants of some of those satellite cones can still be seen, such as 8,900-foot Mount Scott.

The character of lava beneath Mount Mazama began to change. Extrusions from fissures far down the slopes from the summit have been identified. Some of these lava flows

(Following pages) Glacier Peak, at 10,451 feet, is so named because of the numerous glaciers that can be seen from its summit. Her last volcanic activity occurred approximately 12,500 years ago.

131

were as much as 1,000 feet thick. Embedded in the many layers of volcanic and glacial deposits in the region are huge chunks of lava, suggesting that between long periods of relative quiescence, Mount Mazama erupted with extreme violence. At its maximum Mount Mazama may have reached an elevation of 12,000 feet.

By 6,600 years ago, forests covered the mountain's lower slopes and Indians lived in its shadows.

Geologists have created a scenario of what the ultimate eruption must have been like. That period of volcanic activity probably began with ''minor'' eruptions of ash and pumice that were carried as far as present-day central Oregon. Succeeding eruptions, increasing in intensity, left a layer of ash 20 feet deep near the peak, one foot deep 70 miles away. In a rain of fire, pumice was piled up to 50 feet in depth, where the pumice desert, north of Crater Lake, lies today. As much as an inch of pumice originating from Mount Mazama has been identified at Saskatchewan, 600 miles north. Hot ash avalanches traveled down river valleys; one reached a distance of 40 miles. So much material was expelled, about 15 cubic miles, that the mountain simply collapsed in on itself.

But the mountain began to rebuild. Wizard Island is the cinder cone of a new, young volcano that grew amid the ruins of the old one. It is possible that Mount Mazama will erupt again someday. The peak has a history of long quiet periods. Volcanic activity could take the form of development of new satellite cones or eruptions from Wizard Island. Lava might seep from fissures around the flanks or pumice could be shot into the air. It could begin tomorrow, or it could be at rest for centuries. No one knows.

The Sisters and Family

If all the volcanoes, long dormant, recently dormant, or considered extinct, in a 25-mile stretch of the Cascades, midway through Oregon, were to start belching steam all at once, a high-flying observer would be sure he had been transported to an alien planet.

Dominating the skyline in a whole family of cones, buttes, craters, and summits are the Three Sisters. Among the rest of the ''family'' are Bachelor Butte, Broken Top, Husband, Wife, Little Brother, Belknap Crater, Mount Washington, and several lesser cones, every one of them a volcano. The entire area is a veritable volcanic wonderland of some of the infinite varieties of terrain that can be created through

millenia of eruptions, extrusions, erosion, lava flows, and ash and pumice deposits.

During the 1920s a popular theory prevailed that five of the peaks, including the North Sister, were fragments of a caldera wall left when an ancient volcano, Mount Multnomah, exploded. This theory has been discredited today, because each of the five mountains shows evidence of independent volcanic activity.

Broken Top

Broken Top is a shield volcano with a cinder cone as the upper story. Most of what is left of Broken Top, today, is its core, a fascinating, colorful stack of layers of assorted volcanic and glacial deposits. The cinder cone mountain, which once existed, has been largely worn away by erosion. Broken Top began life quietly, but later was explosive, tossing out lava bombs eight feet long. Deposits from incendiary flows are found over a 200-square-mile area.

Bachelor Butte

Bachelor Butte is most well known for the popular ski resort complex on its northern side. It is southernmost of the Sisters family and possibly one of the youngest of the volcanoes. It is remarkably symmetrical and little eroded, so that geologists think the visible cone may have been built since the last glacial period, which ended 10,000 years ago. Ash from Mount Mazama's blast 6,600 years ago overlays the uneroded basalt, so it would seem the butte rose sometime between seven and ten thousand years ago. There are parasitic cones about the base that may be more recent. One small glacier provides an interesting laboratory for observing how glaciers erode the rock beneath them. Basalt is a hard, dense rock, yet, where this small ice field grinds away at the butte's slopes, basalt is worn away to a fine, powdery dust.

History of the region would indicate such a young cone is still in the building stage. While there is no indication of imminent eruptions, there are several hot spots where snow regularly melts. If Bachelor Butte develops similarly to some of the other volcanoes in the region, it may not erupt explosively, but simply extrude lava flows from fissures in its sides.

Belknap Crater, South Belknap, Little Belknap, and Yapoah

The narrow, winding road through McKenzie Pass, between Eugene and Bend, traverses a 70-square-mile area of lava beds. Less than 3,000 years ago, Little Belknap and Yapoah Cinder Cone emitted lava flows that engulfed two older volcanic cones, leaving just their tops exposed, little "islands" among the lava rocks. Again, 1,800 years ago and 1,500 years ago, major flows streamed out of Little Belknap, the more recent one flowing west until it plunged into the McKenzie River valley, where it changed the course of the river.

Belknap Crater is a 6,869-foot cinder cone that, at one time, erupted enough ash to scatter it over 100 square miles. South Belknap and Little Belknap are actually vents on the sides of Belknap. The volcanic products of this group, and over 100 other separate volcanic vents just north of North Sister, have left a jumbled, lava rock desert.

North Sister

Climbers tackling North Sister find almost sheer cliffs as they approach the summit, thus this Sister is considered the most difficult of the three to climb. The 10,085-foot peak is the oldest of the family and tremendously eroded.

Similar to Broken Top, the North Sister began as a quietly built basalt shield, and, as eruptions became explosive, a cone was built on top of the shield. From the cone a series of thin lava flows were issued. In one place, where a cross section is exposed, a 120-foot-high cliff can be seen which contains at least 50 separate layers.

It is speculated that at its zenith North Sister may have been 11,000 feet in elevation, but erosion carved away almost 1,000 feet. In its later development lava intruded into many fissures in the slopes and solidified. These lava dikes have been exposed after centuries of erosion and are the verticle walls that radiate from the summit. There is a plug left from the main conduit that is 300 yards wide and forms the two summit pinnacles.

Middle Sister

At 10,047 feet high, wearing a snow robe the year round, the Middle Sister, sitting in the shadow of her sisters, is indeed a middle child with no special place in the family. In most other places in the United States, the Middle Sister would be an outstanding peak, subject to the romance and lore of most of our country's snow-covered mountains.

This Sister's geologic history closely parallels that of other mountains in the region—a cone built on a basalt base. The eastern face of the cone has been eroded away, but there are no spectacular lava dikes to leave astonishing formations. Neither had Middle Sister erupted in recent history to create a crater.

South Sister

One of South Sister's most intriguing features is its "now you see it, now you don't" little crater lake. At the 10,358-foot summit there is an almost perfectly round crater. During warm weather when the snow melts, the crater holds a small lake—the highest body of water in Oregon.

The broad base of South Sister may be contemporaneous with that of North Sister. Upon that firm foundation, later volcanism built a lava cone.

Numerous eruptions and lava flows, emitted through several vents and fissures at many different times in the mountain's history, built a complex structure of several kinds of rock. Some lava flows were extremely viscuous and did not flow away, but piled up in heaps that were later fractured into jumbled piles of obsidian by the pressure of more lava rising from beneath.

Erosion has been a major factor in the shaping and molding of South Sister. At least three times glaciers have covered or almost covered the area.

Of the Three Sisters, it seems that South Sister may have erupted most recently. The summit crater appears to be fairly fresh. Since this part of Oregon is sparsely populated and settled only recently, such an eruption may not have been observed.

Others in the Family

Unless one were to devote an entire book to this one small area of the Cascades, it would be of no purpose to mention every one of the many cones, summits, and buttes around the Sisters. But some are notable for some reason or another. The Husband, the Wife, Sphinx, and Burnt Top all have features similar to North Sister and likely developed around the same time. An interesting formation of four clustered, nearly identical cinder cones is called, logically enough, "Four-in-One-Cone." Collier Cone may be the most recent peak in the area to erupt lava. It has a compli-

Mt. Garibaldi in British Columbia is currently thought to be extinct, lacking signs of internal heat.

Mt. Adams as seen from Larch Mountain, Oregon.

cated history of volcanic activity and produced the square-mile desolated Ahalapam Cinder Field.

Sisters Area Today

The wilderness area surrounding the Three Sisters is a major mountain recreational area. In addition to skiing at Bachelor Butte, there are hiking trails and campgrounds. A drive on the Cascade Lakes Highway southwest from Bend in central Oregon will bring the visitor to many of the 37 lakes in the region and provide views of a countless number of striking mountain landscapes. These mountains are in the lee of the Cascades and this country is higher and drier than that on the western slope. The sky is strikingly blue, the air almost unbelievably clear.

In an area totally buried in lava, pumice, and ash, dotted with the remains of hundreds of volcanic vents, it seems impossible that all volcanic activity has ceased. Perhaps here, more than anywhere else in the Cascades, the potential exists for the creation of another brand-new mountain.

Mount Adams

In Indian legend Pahto fought Wy'east over the affections of Lawetlatla. The adversaries threw fire across the skies and belched smoke to the heavens.

The Indians didn't understand the mechanics of volcanoes but they were awed by the pyrotechnics. Surely these fire-breathing mountains were gods, or the servants of gods.

In the war between these two giants, the bridge across a mighty river was destroyed. The river was the Columbia. Today we call Wy'east Mount Hood, Lawetlatla Mount St. Helens, and Pahot is Mount Adams.

Mount Adams lies approximately 40 miles east of Mount St. Helens on the eastern flank of the Cascades in southern Washington. At a 12,286-foot elevation, this peak is the second highest in Washington and Oregon, surpassed only by Mount Rainier. It is broad, flat-topped, and remote, accessible only by unpaved roads. Probably because there are other lovely mountains closer to major northwest centers of population, Mount Adams has not been developed for recreation at all. However, its unique mineral deposits, sulfur, alum, and gypsum, attracted commercial exploitation. For 30 years sulfur was mined from the crater and carried down the south slope by horses and mules.

Mount Adams' geologic history has not been as well studied as that of many other Cascade peaks, possibly because it is so inaccessible, or possibly because there just is not that much interest in the solitary mountain. It is a composite cone, but it is thought to be a collection of several cones rather than the eroded remains of just one.

There seems to be no evidence of exceptional violence; rather, lava flows were apparently the principal kind of volcanic activity that built the mountain. A recent flow on the south side may be no more than 2,000 years old. Apart from the superimposed complex of cinder cones that comprise the main peak, Adams has numerous parasitic cones. Two of them, Little Mount Adams and Potato Hill, remain so far uneroded.

Evidence of current volcanic activity is sparse. Indian tales suggest that sometime since the tribes have inhabited the Northwest, Adams has erupted at least smoke. Sulfurous gasses emit from fissures about the crater and climbers regularly report a strong sulfur smell at the summit.

It was a climbing party that had reached the top of Mount Adams that had a real box seat for the May 18 eruption of Mount St. Helens. Members of the group reported sparks from ice axes, ink-black sky, a 15-degree rise in temperature, and a rain of ash, rock, and other debris. The usually white mountain was left grey in the summer of 1980 with a coating of dark ash.

Mount Baker

Until Mount St. Helens' present eruptive cycle commenced, the most volcanic activity in the Cascades was taking place on Mount Baker, northernmost high peak of the United States Cascades.

Like Mount St. Helens, Mount Baker had a history of eruption in the last century, and in this one it had been steaming almost continually from a number of vents in the main crater. In 1975 thermal activity increased and melted through 150 feet of ice. Melted ice and snow formed a small lake in the crater. Later that year the lake drained from the crater into, or beneath, a glacier on the east side. Officials were concerned about avalanches and closed some areas of the mountain, particularly around Baker Lake. No more significant activity has been observed since then, but Mount Baker is watched closely by science.

The North Cascades are deeply folded and uplifted and far more rugged than the southern part of the range. Atop this serrated landscape sits a young stratovolcano, 10,750 feet high. Lying in one of the highest rainfall areas of the country, this mountain accumulates an annual snowfall of 80 feet, so it is the most heavily glaciated of all the Cascade volcanoes. Mount Baker's eruptive activity began two miles west of the present summit at the Black Buttes. The original vent was the source of several flows of thin, fluid lava that spread out to build a broad base for the main cone.

Because it is so heavily glaciated, yet shows so much less evidence of glacial erosion than peaks with less glacial ice, it is thought that the present cone is comparatively young. Layers of lava flows, pyroclastics, and ash show that regular activity has occurred to the present. The main crater is in a depression between two summits that may be the remnants of an older, higher crater wall. The crater is the site of steam caves similar to those found on Mount Rainier.

A series of eruptions during the 1800s, contemporaneous with those of Mount St. Helens, have been well documented. Like those people who reported about St. Helens, the individual writers sometimes do not agree exactly on dates. Probably the most reliable report is of an eruption in 1854. A scientist was observing Mount Baker ''through a glass'' when he saw ''vast rolling masses of dense smoke.'' Bad weather obscured night observation so the reporter could not see if there was any glow.

In 1854 people in Victoria, British Columbia, saw clouds brilliantly aglow with light from an eruption. Periodic eruptions continued into the 1860s.

The major concern today, in the event of increased volcanic activity, is glacial melt, which would cause snow avalanches and mudslides. While a major explosive eruption of any volcano is very destructive, few of the Cascade mountains have the quantity of stored water that Mount Baker has.

Mount Jefferson

Leaning on the railing overlooking Metolius Springs, where a river flows full blown from a cleft in a rock, one sees a lush green marsh and behind it a jagged, snow-covered peak, picture postcard sharp in crisp, clean air. Singularly, strikingly beautiful, from this vista southeast of it, Mount Jefferson is sharp and angular.

From its appearance one would think Mount Jefferson was formed in the same way as other similarly pointed mountains, such as Thielsen or Washington. But this is not so. These others are lava dikes left after the surrounding cone was worn away. Jefferson's shape is the happy accident of the sequence of lava eruptions and erosion.

Mount Jefferson is 10,495 feet high, the second highest mountain in Oregon and located 40 miles south of the highest, Mount Hood. It had violent beginnings in a series of explosive eruptions that left a classic cone. That original cone was subsequently buried under sheets of basalt that flowed away from the main vent, leaving thin layers high on

the peak and piling up to as much as 2,000 feet farther away. Following the time when this first lava eroded, additional lava flows, thicker and more sluggish, were emitted. After this period of lava buildup, the mountain may have reached an altitude of 12,000 feet. New glaciation and its severe scouring wore away almost all the western part of the early mountain and over 1,500 feet from the summit.

As do most of the other volcanoes near it, Mount Jefferson has satellite cones and at one time lava issued from fissures in its slopes.

Compared to other Cascade volcanoes, Mount Jefferson has had a rather mundane past. It has not had any especially explosive period when it distributed ash over a large area, nor has it erupted a particularly large amount of lava. There is no evidence of any volcanic activity for the past 10,000 years, and there are no hot spots of any kind today. Thus Mount Jefferson can be considered an extinct volcano.

Some Lesser Known Cascade Volcanoes
Glacier Peak, Mt. Thielsen, Mt. McLoughlin, and Newberry Crater

Southern Oregon's Mount McLoughlin, 70 miles north of Mount Shasta, is the severely eroded remainder of a symmetrical peak that possibly may have been 10,000 feet high at its maxim.

It lies at the southern terminus of the huge sheet of ice that buried its northern neighbors during the last glacial period. The northeast face of this peak has been sharply carved away, leaving an interesting cross section of the composition of the slopes. The mountain appears to be a cinder cone sheathed in layers of lava. There is no evidence of any volcanic activity for at least 1,500 years.

Lonely and isolated, clad in the ice armor that gives it its name, Glacier Peak lies in the north Cascades, just west of the divide, in an area inaccessible by vehicle or even casual hikers. It dates back less than a million years and was built, primarily, of quiet lava flows. There is no evidence of any eruptions during the last 12,000 years, but during the last period of activity, Glacier Peak issued large quantities of ash that left identifiable layers as far away as Montana.

Mount Thielsen, at 9,178 feet, is one of four similar mountains that are much older volcanoes than the others considered in this volume. The other three are Union Peak, Mount Washington, and Three-Fingered Jack. All are in

Newberry Volcano, south of Bend, Oregon, contains Paulina and East Lakes.
Pictured here is Paulina Lake. Sections of this volcano were used as
training grounds for the astronauts before their lunar landing.

Mt. Jefferson, 40 miles south of Mt. Hood, rises to a height of 10,495 feet,
and is now thought to be extinct.

Oregon and all are pinnacles reminiscent of Switzerland's famous Matterhorn.

Mount Thielsen's story is representative of the birth, growth, and erosion of them all. This mountain began as a basalt shield volcano, which, eventually, erupted explosively, building a cone atop the shield. Into the vent and adjoining fissures rose heavy lava that solidified into lava dikes, much harder and denser than the surrounding fragmental material—and two huge, half-mile-wide plugs at the cone. Erosion stripped away the fragmental materials leaving the lava plugs and dikes exposed.

While not technically a part of the Cascades, Newberry Crater is an interesting formation in the broad volcanic area in central Oregon. Like Mount Mazama, Newberry is the remnant of a much larger mountain, but unlike Mazama it collapsed into its magma chamber after all the lava had seeped out around its base. The area continues to be geologically active. The broad, cinder-cone dotted Newberry Shield is sometimes referred to as the Paulina Mountains, after a peak on the crater's south rim that is the highest point, and one of the crater's two lakes. The East Lake fissure is a 20-mile-long fault, with one end at the Newberry caldera rim, and the other near Lava Butte, a recent cinder cone. These two formations, Newberry Crater and Lava Butte, are excellent examples of the works of volcanism in the midst of a land that is in the process of building.

Beautiful America Publishing Company

The nation's foremost publisher of quality color photography

Current Books

Alaska
Arizona
Boston
British Columbia
California
California Vol. II
California Coast
California Desert
California Missions
California Mountains
Chicago
Colorado
Dallas
Delaware
Denver
Florida
Georgia
Hawaii
Idaho
Illinois
Indiana
Kentucky
Las Vegas
Los Angeles, 200 Years

Maryland
Massachusetts
Michigan
Michigan Vol. II
Minnesota
Missouri
Montana
Montana Vol. II
Monterey Peninsula
Mormon
Mt. Hood (Oregon)
Nevada
New Jersey
New Mexico
New York
New York City
Northern California
Northern California Vol. II
North Carolina
North Idaho
Ohio
Oklahoma
Orange County
Oregon

Oregon Vol. II
Oregon Coast
Oregon Country
Pacific Coast
Pennsylvania
Pittsburgh
San Diego
San Francisco
San Juan Islands
Seattle
Tennessee
Texas
Utah
Utah Country
Vancouver U.S.A.
Vermont
Virginia
Volcano Mt. St. Helens
Washington
Washington Vol. II
Washington, D.C.
Wisconsin
Wyoming
Yosemite National Park

Forthcoming Books

Alabama
Arkansas
Baltimore
Connecticut
Detroit
The Great Lakes
Houston
Kansas

Kauai
Maine
Maui
Mississippi
New England
New Hampshire
North Dakota

Oahu
Phoenix
Rhode Island
Rocky Mountains
South Carolina
South Dakota
West Virginia

Large Format, Hardbound Books

Beautiful America
Beauty of California
Beauty of Oregon

Beauty of Washington
Glory of Nature's Form
Volcanoes of the West

Lewis & Clark Country
Western Impressions

Enlarged Prints

Most of the photography in this book is available as photographic
enlargements. Send self-addressed, stamped envelope for information.
For a complete product catalog, send $1.00.
Beautiful America Publishing Company
P.O. Box 608
Beaverton, Oregon 97075